This paper is part of the
Proceedings
of the
Second North-American Conference on Semitic Linguistics
Santa Barbara, California
March 25-26, 1974

VERB COMPLEMENTS AND RELATIVE CLAUSES
A DIACHRONIC CASE STUDY IN BIBLICAL HEBREW [1]

Talmy Givón
Department of Linguistics
University of California, Los Angeles

A diachronic development in Biblical Hebrew is studied by which the relative subordinating particle *še* becomes also a verb-complement subordinator. It is argued (a) that this development is internally motivated and is not the result of borrowing; and (b) that the development is not the result of simple-minded analogy. Rather, two natural mediating channels are discussed which, it is felt, are responsible for this syntactic change. It is also suggested that a similar development may have taken place in Aramaic (*di*) and Akkadian (*ša*).

TABLE OF CONTENTS

---

[1] I am indebted to Robert Hetzron, Joe Malone and Stanislav Segert for stimulating discussion and many helpful comments. The opinions expressed below remain strictly my own.

1. INTRODUCTION

In Modern Hebrew, Biblical Aramaic, Akkadian, English, Spanish and no doubt a great number of other languages, the same subordinating morpheme introduces both relative clauses and sentential complements of cognition and utterance verbs (i.e.'say', 'know'). The most facile explanation that usually comes to mind, is that the similarity is the result of ANALOGICAL EXTENSION. That is, that the subordinator morpheme belonged originally to only one of the two constructions, and was later extended by analogy to the other. There are a number of reasons why one should feel uncomfortable with this type of explanation. For one thing, it makes inordinately strong claims about the nature of the 'syntactic intuition' of the speakers, and in particular of children acquiring their first language.[2] What I hope to show here is that the analogy hypothesis is not only *a priori* suspect but also unnecessary given the data of one specific language.

Of the array of subordinating morphemes shared by relative clauses and verb complements, one may distinguish between two general types. The first involves INTERROGATIVE pronouns, such as the Spanish *que*. This pattern will be largely excluded from the present discussion. The other pattern involves most often DEMONSTRATIVE pronouns, such as the English *that*, Aramaic *di*, Archaic

[2]As I have suggested in Givón (1974), the assumption of analogy here would be tantamount to a claim that speakers analogize in language along Chomsky's $\bar{X}$ CONVENTION. That is, that they possess a syntactic categorization HEAD: COMPLEMENT whether for noun phrases or verb phrases. I think this a much too powerful assumption, particularly since it is most likely that there is a great disparity in the time and manner of acquisition of verb complementation and noun complementation by children.

Biblical Hebrew *zu* or the Akkadian *ša*. Whether inflected or uninflected for case, these morphemes appear rather universally as relative-subordinators or relative-PRONOUNS. The Biblical Hebrew subordinator *ʔašer* (and its later contracted form *še-*) is not etymologically an ex-demonstrative, but nevertheless it falls within this general type. In Early Biblical Hebrew (henceforth EBH) *ʔašer* appears only as a relative subordinator. In Mishnaic Hebrew (2nd century AD) *še-* is both the relative and verb-complement subordinator. The diachronic direction of spreading—relative clause to verb complement—is thus well established. As I will show later on, the etymological relationship between *ʔašer* and *še-* is also well supported by both internal and comparative considerations. What I hope to show below is that rather suggestive intermediate stages may be found in the syntax of Biblical Hebrew, some in EBH and more frequently in the Late Books, so that the spreading of this subordinator to verb complements may be viewed as a natural ('organic') development within the language, comprising of a number of SPECIFIC semantic-syntactic extensions, rather than an overall 'analogy'. This development in Biblical Hebrew may be highly relevant to the study of other languages exhibiting the same double-function of the subordinator. It may also shed some light on the general process of developing a category 'verb S-complement' in language.

2. RELATIVE CLAUSES IN EARLY BIBLICAL HEBREW

The dialect level defined for the purpose of this discussion involves mostly the language of Genesis, Joshua and Judges. The discussion involves mainly a general background for the main topic of the paper, and more specifically the gradual spreading of *ʔašer* into the relative clause paradigm. In addition to the patterns discussed in some detail below, another one, designated here as the Archaic Biblical Hebrew (ABH) is also attested. This pattern involves the use of the uninflected *zu* (etymologically an offshoot of the DEMONSTRATIVE series) as a relative subordinator. As I shall argue further below, this pattern is the exact equivalent of the Aramaic *di*, except that in ABH the morpheme *zu* is attested only as a relative-clause subordinator, while the Aramaic *di* is also used to subordinate sentential complements of verbs. In this section I will discuss the three major patterns of relativization in EBH.

2.1. The *ʔašer* pattern

This pattern, clearly the major one in EBH, involves the use of the subordinator *ʔašer* either between the head noun and the relative clause or—when the head noun undergoes anaphoric or diachronic[4] deletion—as the anaphoric head of the construction. This pattern is distributed in the following environments:

---

[3]The transcription used below for citing data from Biblical Hebrew is somewhat simplified toward Modern Hebrew pronounciation of the text. This involves mostly the use of a five-vowel system, the dispensing with geminated consonants (*dagesh*) except in /k/, /p/ and /b/ where the value of the pronounced consonant is altered, the use of [v] to indicate both the 'weak' /β/ and consonantal /w/, and the dispensing with a stop/spirant distinction for /g/ and /d/. I have used the symbols /ʔ/ for א, /ᶜ/ for ע, /h/ for ה, /ḥ/ for ח, /q/ for ק, /ṣ/ for צ, /x/ for כ, /s/ for ס, /ś/ for שׂ, /š/ for שׁ and /ṭ/ for ט.

[4]A frequent anaphoric usage of *ʔašer*, often with a preposition, may be exemplified in constructions such as:

ʔet	*ʔašer*	*ᶜaśa*	'(the thing) that he did', 'what he did'
ACC	THAT	he-did	
kol	*ʔašer*	*yavoʔ*	'(the person) that comes', 'whoever comes'
all	THAT	comes	
ba-ʔašer	*telxi*		'to (the place) that you go', 'wherever you go'
at-THAT	you-will-go		
ᶜad	*ʔašer*	*yavoʔ*	'until (the time) that the comes', 'till he comes'
till	THAT	he-comes	

2.1.1. RELATIVE-SUBJECT OF COPULAR CONSTRUCTIONS

(1) *ha-bhemah* *ʔašer* *ʔito* *ba-tevah* (Gen. 8.1)
the-beast THAT with-him in-the-ark
'the animals that were with him in the ark'

(2) *ʔašer* *ʕal* *pney* *ha-ʔareṣ* (Gen. 1.29)
THAT on face-of the-earth
'that is on the face of the earth'

(3) *kol* *ʔašer* *la-hem* (Joshua 2.14)
all THAT to-them
'all that is to them', 'all that they have/had'

The *ʔašer* construction is obligatory in these constructions. That is, they may not be relativized via any other pattern. Example (3) above also represents the GENITIVE pattern with *ʔašer*, which is an extension of this COPULAR-LOCATIVE pattern.

2.1.2. RELATIVE-SUBJECT OF NEGATIVE PARTICIPIALS/ADJECTIVALS

The affirmative counterparts of these are ordinarily relativized in EBH via the definitizer *ha-* pattern, see below. However, the corresponding negatives appear obligatorily in the *ʔašer* pattern:

(4) *ha-bhemah* *ʔašer* *loʔ* *ṭhorah* (Gen. 7.2)
the-beast THAT not pure
'the beast that is not pure'

(5) *ha-bhemah* *ʔašer* *ʔen-enah* *ṭhorah* (Gen. 7.8)
the-beast THAT no-she pure
'the beast that is not pure'

2.1.3. RELATIVE-SUBJECT OF VERBS IN THE PERFECT AND IMPERFECT

While the morphological Perfect and Imperfect paradigms must take the *ʔašer* pattern in subject relativization, the very same SEMANTIC contents may be rendered with equal ease via the other two major patterns.[5] The significance of this observation will be discussed further below.

Further, I would like to consider expressions such as:

ka-ʔašer *ʕasa* '(the manner) that he did', 'like/as he did'
like-THAT he-did

as well as similar expressions in purpose, reason and other 'adverbial' clauses, as diachronic development along this anaphora pattern, i.e. where the underlying head noun 'manner', 'purpose', 'reason' etc. is deleted by convention—though the specific preposition most often has been retained.

[5]Particularly when the expression is generic/habitual, one may chose either the perfect, imperfect or participial ('present') as the verb form, and the latter allows the *ha-* relativization pattern. Thus the proposition 'whoever goes' may be rendered as:

kol *ha-holex* (participial)
all THE-walking

kol *ʔašer* *yhalex* (imperfect)
all THAT goes

kol *ʔašer* *halax* (perfect)
all THAT went

The latter (perfect) is of course appropriate only in environments subordinated to the past or perfect aspect.

Some examples of this pattern are:

(6) *ha-ʔadamah ʔašer paṣtah ʔet piha* (Gen. 4.11)
the-earth THAT opened ACC her-mouth
'the earth that opened its mouth'

(7) *ki ʔim ʔašer yeṣeʔ mi-meʕexa* (Gen. 15.4)
but if THAT will-come-out from-your-bowels
'except for (the one) that will come out of your flesh'

(8) *mi-kol maʔaxal ʔašer yeʔaxel* (Gen. 6.21)
from all food THAT will-be-eaten
'of all the food that may be eaten'

Example (8) above represents the subject of a passivized verb, which falls into this paradigm as long as the verb is in the Perfect or Imperfect form.

2.1.4. OBJECT RELATIVIZATION

In addition to the accusative, dative and locative objects of verbs, I am also including here the various 'adverbial' clauses, such as time, place, manner, purpose etc.

(a) ACCUSATIVE

(9) *mlaxto ʔašer ʕašah* (Gen. 2.2)
work-his THAT he-did
'the work that he did'

(10) *ha-ʔareṣ ʔašer ʔarʔe-xa* (Gen. 12.1)
the-land THAT I-will-show-you
'the land that I will show you'

(b) DATIVE

(11) *ʔet ha-ʕir ʔašer dibarta* (Gen. 19.21)
ACC the-town THAT you-talked
'the town about which you talked'

(c) LOCATIVE

(12) *ha-maqom ʔašer tidrox kaf ragl-xa b-o* (Joshua 1.3)
the-place THAT will-step sole foot-of-you in-it
'the place where your foot will step'

(13) *b-xol ʔašer telex* (Joshua 1.9)
at-all THAT you-will-go
'wherever you go'

(14) *ha-bašar ʔašer b-o ruaḥ ḥayim* (Gen. 7.15)
the-flesh THAT in-it spirit of life
'the flesh in which dwells the spirit of life'

(d) MANNER

(15) *k-xol ʔašer šamaʕnu el Moše* (Joshua 1.17)
like-all THAT we-listened to Moses
'just as we listened to Moses'

(16) *ka-ʔašer hayah ʕim Moše* (Joshua 1.17)
like-THAT he-was with Moses
'the way he was with Moses'

(e) TIME

(17) *ka-ʔašer hiqriv lavoʔ miṣraymah* (Gen. 12.11)
as-THAT he-neared to-come Egypt-LOC
'when he approached Egypt'

(18) *ʔaxarey ʔašer hafax yisraʔel ᶜoref* (Joshua 7.8)
after-of THAT turned Israel (its) neck
'after Israel turned their back'

(19) *ᶜad ʔašer heḥrim* (Joshua 8.26)
till THAT he-destroyed
'until he destroyed'

(f) PURPOSE

(20) *l-maᶜan ʔašer yṣaveh* (Gen. 18.19)
for-reason THAT he-orders
'so that he will order'

As will be shown further below, the same SEMANTIC contents of the adverbial clauses above, in particular those of time, manner and purpose, may be expressed by the genitive-nominal relativization pattern just as well.

2.2. The Participial-Adjectival Pattern with *ha-*

This pattern is limited in EBH to adjectival constructions, many of which may be participial derivatives of verbs, most normally conveying the sense of 'present progressive' or 'habitual present'. Whenever the head of such a construction is DEFINITE, as is obviously the case with most relative modification, the modifier-participial itself also takes the definitizer *ha-*, as is the case in general with adjectives in Hebrew. Thus:

(21) *kol ᶜešev zoreaᶜ zeraᶜ* (Gen. 1.29)
all grass seeding seed
'all the grass that seeds (its) seed'

(22) *kol ha-basar ha-romeš* (Gen. 7.21)
all THE-flesh THE-crawling
'all the animals that crawl'

Thus the definitizer *ha-* is not really a relative subordinator here. This is basically a JUXTAPOSED pattern, which is the normal one for adjectives. Only when the (definite) head noun is anaphorically deleted does *ha-* appear as the 'subordinator' of the construction, as in:

(23) *v-ha-ʔorev qam mherah mi-mqomo* (Joshua 8.19)
and-THE-ambushing stood quickly from-his-place
'and those (who were) ambushing stood up quickly'

2.3. The genitival-nominal pattern

This pattern involves the NOMINALIZATION of the underlying verb of the embedded ('relative') sentence, after which that de-verbal noun appears as a GENITIVE modifier of the head noun. It is not a discernible pattern with SUBJECT relatives, where the adjectival pattern (2.2. above) is its close equivalent (seeing that in Hebrew the participial de-verbal may be interpreted equally well as 'adjectival' or 'nominal', both of which share the same gender-and-number agreement pattern[6]). The following example may be thus considered a genitival-nominal pattern for subject relativization:

(24) *ᶜeṣ pri ᶜošeh pri* (Gen. 1.11)
tree-of fruit DOING-OF fruit
'fruit tree which bears fruit'

---

[6] One may further argue that the category ADJECTIVE does not really exist in (Early Biblical) Hebrew as a formal category distinct from a NOMINALIZATION of the verb. The participial form of the verb takes the nominal number-gender suffixes and exhibits the appropriate genitival stem-form as do all other nouns.

Non-participial nominalizations may be also used in EBH, but for subject, accusative and locative 'relativization' these are very clearly petrified LEXICAL patterns, rather than syntactic/synchronic ones. Thus:

(a) SUBJECT

(25) *ha-mʔorot* *ha-gdolim* (Gen. 1.16)
the-LIGHTERS the-big
'the big lights'

(26) *l-memšelet* *ha-yom* (Gen. 1.16)
to-GOVERNMENT-of the-day
'for governing the day'

(b) ACCUSATIVE OBJECT

(27) *ʔimrey* *pi* (Deut. 32.1)
SAYINGS-OF my-mouth
'what I say'

(28) *mi-švuᶜat-ex* *ʔašer* *nišbaᶜt-anu* (Joshua 2.20)
from-PROMISE-yours that you-swore-us
'of the oath which you swore to us'

(c) LOCATIVE OBJECT

Here one could cite the following derived nominals, all with the nominalizing prefix *m*-, and all lexical:

(29) *morad* 'down-slope', from **yrd* 'go down'
maᶜaleh 'up-slope', from **ᶜl(h)* 'go up'
maqom 'place', from **qwm* 'stand'
mošav 'sitting place', from **yšv* 'sit'

Where the pattern becomes highly productive, synchronically, is primarily in time-clauses, where the INFINITIVAL nominalization is used[7]:

(d) TIME CLAUSES

(30) *b-yom* *ᶜašot* *YHWH* (Gen. 2.4)
in-day-of DOING-OF God
'on the day when God made'

Most commonly the head-noun ('day', 'time', 'year', 'hour' etc.) of the construction is missing ('anaphorically deleted'), so that the nominalized verb follows directly the time preposition, as in:

(31) *b-hibarʔam* (Gen. 2.4)
in-BEING-CREATED-OF-THEM
'when they were created'

(32) *ᶜad* *šuv-xa* *ʔel* *ha-ʔadama* (Gen. 3.19)
till RETURNING-your to the-earth
'until you return to the earth'

---

[7]As a rule of thumb one may say that the INFINITIVAL nominalization in a language is the 'least lexical' and 'most syntactic' nominalized form of the verb. This may be expressed in terms of PRODUCTIVITY: This is the only nominalization that is fully-productive, and is thus not constrained by special idiosyncracies of individual lexical items. In contrast, the *m*-nominalizations, even in EBH, are a rather mixed, irregular bag, yielding locatives (*maqom* 'place'), instrumentals (*maᶜader* 'hoe'), agents (*memšalah* 'government') and probably others. The *m*- prefix in subject-agentives of the *piᶜel* conjugation in the participial-present, such as *m-lamed* 'the one who teaches', may be also viewed as an off-shoot of this pattern.

(33) *ˀaxar-ey holid-o ˀet Mahalˀel* (Gen. 5.13)
after-of SIRING-his ACC Mahalel
'after he sired Mahalel'

(34) *ki-šmoaᶜ malxey ha-ˀemori* (Joshua 5.1)
as-HEARING-of kings-of the-Emorite
'when the Emorite kings heard'

Though rarely, the same pattern may be also found in purpose clauses:

(e) PURPOSE CLAUSES

(35) *l-maᶜan haḥrim-am* (Joshua 11.20)
for-reason-of DESTROYING-their
'in order that they destroy'

Finally, in manner clauses the LEXICAL (i.e. non-infinitival) nominalization is again found (with the prefix *m-*):

(f)

(36) *yrušah k-maḥlqot-am* (Joshua 12.7)
inheritance as-DIVISIONS-their
'inheritance according to their divisions'

Though the non-lexical pattern, with an INFINITIVAL nominalization, may also be observed, as in:

(37) *ki-lḥox ha-šor ˀet yereq ha-šadeh* (Num. 22.4)
as-CHEWING-of the-ox ACC grass-of the-field
'(the way) the ox chews the grass of the field'

In the next section the numerical distribution of the three relativization patterns, together with its implications, will be considered.

2.4. The Distribution of Relativization Patterns in Early Biblical Hebrew

Whenever syntactic options are available for the expression of the very same semantic contents, the numerical distribution of the various patterns may be of great interest. The data below pertain, first, to the first 20 chapters of Genesis.

TABLE 1 (Genesis)

	ˀašer	PARTICIPIAL	GENITIVAL[8]
SUBJECT	9	19	(5)
ACCUSATIVE OBJECT	32	Ø	(8)
SUBJECT OF COPULAR-PREDICATES	29	Ø	Ø
LOCATIVE OBJECT	11	Ø	(3)
TIME CLAUSE	2	Ø	41
MANNER CLAUSE	9	Ø	(1)
PURPOSE CLAUSE	1	Ø	2

Given this distribution, the following tentative hypothesis may be advanced:

(a) The genitive-nominal pattern of relativization is clearly the oldest. For the most part it has receded into the lexicon already in EBH, with the most conspicuous survival found in time and purpose clauses.

[8]The numbers in parentheses are LEXICAL nominalizations, see discussion in section 2.3. above, also footnote 7.

(b) The participial pattern is limited to the adjectival 'present' form of the verb and has not extended further.

(c) The *ʔašer* relativization pattern has clearly taken over in most categories. The etymology of *ʔašer* (Aramaic *ʔaθar* 'place') strongly suggests that it entered the paradigm in locative expressions, either locative-copula (where there's no alternative pattern attested at all) or locative objects (where the genitival pattern survives only in a few lexical items).

(d) The *ʔašer* pattern probably spread on to accusative objects first, and later on to subjects (of perfect and imperfect). It is clearly spreading into the adverbial-clause paradigms, but at a differential rate.

The only real competition is exhibited between the *ʔašer* and participial patterns in subject relatives. The fact that the grammar is still hedging there can be perhaps discerned from items such as (38) below, where the *ʔašer* pattern is used, rather exceptionally, with the participial form of the verb:

(38) *kol* *ʔašer* *romeš* (Gen. 7.8)
all THAT crawling
'all that is crawling'

In (39) below a similar blend is somewhat mitigated by the use of the copular **hwh* 'be', thus bringing it closer to the normal *ʔašer* pattern of copular expressions—though without a locative predicate:

(39) *ha-romeš* *ʔašer* *huʔ* *ḥay* (Gen. 9.3)
the-crawling THAT he alive
'the crawling (one) that is alive'

Another 'hedge' may be seen in (40) below, where the participial pattern is rather irregularly used in subject relativization of a verb in the perfective form:

(40) *qṣiney* *ha-milḥamah* *he-halxu* *ito* (Joshua 10.24)
officers-of the-war THE-went with-him
'the officers of war who went with him'

Let us now turn to the distribution of the relative patterns in Joshua.

TABLE 2 (Joshua)

	ʔašer	PARTICIPIAL	GENITIVAL[8]
SUBJECT (perfect and imperfect)	17	20	(5)
ACCUSATIVE OBJECT	42	Ø	Ø
SUBJECT OF COPULAR-PREDICATES	57	Ø	Ø
LOCATIVE OBJECT	12	Ø	(4)
TIME CLAUSE	10	Ø	41
MANNER CLAUSE	41	Ø	2
PURPOSE CLAUSE	1	Ø	4

While I have no statistics to reflect on the significance of the shifts, it seems that whenever the shift is clearly discernible, i.e. in both the SUBJECT (perfect and imperfect) and TIME-CLAUSE paradigms, there is an increase in the *ʔašer* pattern vis-a-vis the participial (subject) and genitival (time-clause) patterns. This certainly is not in conflict with the hypothesis suggested above.

3. VERB COMPLEMENTS IN EARLY BIBLICAL HEBREW

As we shall see further below, in Mishnaic Hebrew the subordinator *še-* —a contracted form of *ʔašer*—is used to introduce both relative clauses and complements of cognition and utterance verbs. The latter function is altogether absent in EBH, though the early precursors of it are already discernible, as will be argued later on.

3.1. Direct and Indirect Quote

The division between direct-quote and indirect-quote verb complements is already present in EBH. the criteria used for deciding what constitutes a direct-quote sentential complement are rather straight forward: When the first and second person pronouns within the complement sentence are DEICTICALLY-ANCHORED to the narrator—rather than to the grammatical subject of the verb dominating the complement—the complement type should be considered INDIRECT QUOTE. In the style of EBH, further, one could make another strong generalization: Indirect quote complements contain only THIRD-PERSON pronouns, but not first or second person pronouns (in the latter I also include the IMPERATIVE form of the verb)" Further, in indirect quote complements, when a third-person pronoun is used, it MAY refer to the grammatical subject of the verb dominating the complement. While in DIRECT quote it may not. Thus, for example:

(41) *va-yedᶜu* *ki* *ᶜarumim* *hem* (Gen. 3.7)
and-they-knew THAT naked THEY
'and THEY$_i$ knew that THEY$_j$ were naked' (they$_i$ = they$_j$)

This rule of thumb is violated only when an indirect-quote complement is embedded within a direct-quote complement. In which case second and first person pronouns (and imperatives) may appear within the indirect-quote complement. However, those are deictically-anchored NOT to the subject of the verb dominating the indirect-quote complement, but rather to the subject of the verb one step above it—which dominates the DIRECT quote. For example:

(42) *va-yiqraʔ* *parᶜoh* *l-ʔavraham* *va-yoʔmer:* (Gen. 12.18)
and-called Pharaoh to-Abraham and-SAID:
'and Pharaoh called to Abraham and said:

"*lamah* *loʔ* *higadta* *li* *ki* *ʔišt-xa* *hiʔ*"
"why no YOU-TOLD me THAT wife-YOUR she"
"Why didn't you tell me that she was your wife?"'

The deictic reference of 'your' in (42) is controlled by Pharaoh, not by Abraham.

With the above exception in mind, one can make the following generalizations concerning verb complementation in EBH.

(a) All COGNITION verbs, i.e. verbs such as 'see', 'hear', 'know', 'understand', 'forget', 'remember', always take INDIRECT-QUOTE complementation. The subordinator is either *ki* or *ve-hineh* ('and lo', 'and there be'). For example:

(43) *va-yarʔ* *ʔelohim* *ki* *ṭov* (Gen. 1.10)
and-saw God THAT good
'and God saw that it was good'

(44) *va-yarʔ* *ve-hineh* *ḥarvu* *pney* *ha-ʔadamah* (Gen. 8.13)
and-he-saw AND-LO dried face-of the-earth
'and he saw that the face of the earth dried up'

In a small number of instances the subordinator *ki* or *vehineh* is preceded by an accusative object, most often the subject nominal of the complement sentence, as in:

(45) *va-yarʔ* *ʔelohim* *ʔet* *ha-ʔor* *ki* *ṭov* (Gen. 1.4)
and-saw God ACC the-light THAT good
'and God saw the light (and) that it was good'

(46) *va-yarʔ* *ʔelohim* *ʔet* *kol* *ʔašer* *ᶜašah* *ve-hineh* *ṭov* *mʔod* (Gen. 1.31)
and-saw God ACC all that he-did AND-LO good very
'and God saw all that he did (and) that it was very good'

The significance of this pattern will be discussed in detail further below, since it is extremely important in understanding how *ʔašer* spread from the relative clause to the verb complement paradigm.

(b) All UTTERANCE verbs, i.e. verbs of communication directed at some DATIVE object ('hearer'), take direct-quote complements. The most common pattern appears without any subordinating morpheme, as in:

(47) *va-yoʔmer ʔelohim: "yhi ʔor* (Gen. 1.3)
and-said God: "be-there light"
'and God said: "There shall be light"'

In a significant number of cases a reflex of the verb *ʔmr 'say' is used as a 'grammaticized' subordinating morpheme of the direct-quote complement. This subordinator may appear in the infinitive form *leʔmor*, as in:

(48) *va-yṣav ʔelohim ʿal ha-ʔadam leʔmor:* (Gen. 2.10)
and-ordered God on the-man TO-SAY:
'and God ordered man thusly:
"mi-kol ʿeṣ ha-gan toʔxel..."
"from-all tree-of the-garden you-eat..."
"You may eat from any of the garden's trees..."'

Alternatively, an inflected, finite form of *ʔmr may be used, as in:

(49) *va-yvarxe-hu va-yoʔmar: "barux ʔavraham..."* (Gen. 14.19)
and-he-blessed-him AND-HE-SAID: "blessed Abraham..."
'and he blessed him and said: "Blessed be Abraham..."'

This situation holds true for both the Genesis dialect (first 34 chapters) and the Joshua and Judges dialect (first 20 chapters of each), with very little variation. Thus in the chapters of Genesis surveyed, 16% of the direct-quote complements were subordinated by either *leʔmor* or *vayoʔmar*[9] (or equivalent inflected forms), and 84% went unmarked, while the Joshua and Judges dialect showed 32% marked and 68% unmarked. I doubt that the difference is statistically significant, though it may represent a shift toward the morphologically-marked form.

In the next short section I will briefly survey the relativization pattern in Mishnaic Hebrew (henceforth MH).

4. RELATIVIZATION IN MISHNAIC HEBREW

In scanning the first 17 chapters of *Zraʿim*,[10] the following situation may be observed:

(a) With only one exception,[11] *ʔašer* had been universally contracted into *še-*.

(b) All PURPOSE CLAUSES employ *še-*.

(c) The same is true for relativization of SUBJECTS OF COPULAR-PREDICATE, ACCUSATIVE OBJECT and LOCATIVE OBJECT.

---

[9]I have not been able to find any factor conditioning the variation between the infinitival (*leʔmor*) and inflected (*va-yoʔmar*) forms of the subordinator.

[10]The Mishna text used for this study is a facsimile of the Kaufmann Mishna, prepared by Dr. George Beer, Prof. of Theology, Heidelberg. The original manuscript is in the Budapest library and the facsimile was made in Jerusalem in 1968.

[11]The sole instance of *ʔaser* found in the 17 chapters scanned was in:

ve-xol he-harim ʔASER *ba-maʿader yeʿadru* (Zraʿim, Peʔa, 2.2)
and-all the-mountains THAT with-hoe will-be-hoed
'and all the mountains that are cultivated by hoe'

(d) As to TIME CLAUSES, the following distribution obtains:
With *še*-: 47
Genitival: 7

(e) As to SUBJECT RELATIVIZATION, the following distribution obtains:
With *še*-: 73
Participial: 34
Others: 1

It seems reasonably clear that the shift to *ʔašer* in the two categories where 'optional variation' was observed in EBH, had been continuing into MH. Arguments for the identity of *še*- with *ʔašer* will be presented further below.

5. VERB COMPLEMENTATION IN MISHNAIC HEBREW

The verb-complementation pattern in MH is roughly identical to that of Modern Hebrew but radically different from what was seen for EBH. The changes from EBH to MH may be summarized as such:

(a) The subordinator *še*- is used in all INDIRECT-QUOTE complements, as in:

(50) *ʔamru lo: limadta-nu še-ʔen mqablin* (Zraᶜim, Braxot, 2.7)
they-told to-him: you-taught-us THAT-no they-receive
'they told him: You taught us that one doesn't receive...'

(51) *ve-nizkar še-huʔ baᶜal qeriʔ* (Zraᶜim, Braxot, 3.5)
and-remembered THAT-he owner-of happening
'and he remembers that he had a wet dream'

(b) Indirect-quote complements are beginning to appear also with verbs of UTTERANCE, but only when a dative-object ('hearer') is not explicitly mentioned, as in:

(52) *ʔamru ᶜalav ᶜal Rabi Ḥaninaʔ bar Dosaʔ* (Zraᶜim, Braxot, 5.5)
they-said about-him about R. Ḥanina b. Dossa
'they said about R. Hanina bar Dossa

še-hayah mitpalel
THAT-he-was praying
that he was praying'

(53) *u-modim še-ʔim hayu raʔšey šurot mᶜoravim* (Zraᶜim, Peʔa, 3.1)
and-they-admit THAT-if were heads-of rows mixed
'and they admit that if the heads of the rows were mixed'

(54) *ʔim ʔamarta bʔomer ʔeḥad še-huʔ ka-gadiš* (Zraᶜim, Peʔa, 6.6)
if you-said about-heap one THAT-it like-'gadish'
'if you said about one heap that it is like a 'gadish''

(c) Finally, all DIRECT-QUOTE complements are UNMARKED by any subordinator, with the complement sentence coming directly after the utterance verb. This is also the pattern in Modern Hebrew.

6. FROM RELATIVE CLAUSE TO VERB COMPLEMENT

In this section I would like to show that the extension of the use of *ʔašer/še*- from relative clauses to verb complements in Hebrew was a gradual, internally-motivated process, dependent neither on direct analogy nor on outside borrowing. I will show, further, that both Late Biblical Hebrew (henceforth LBH) and Mishnaic Hebrew exhibit a number of syntactic intermediates which could shed light on this development. I will also show that a number of these intermediates may be traced back all the way to EBH.

6.1. The Use of *še-* as a Sentence Subordinator in Mishnaic Hebrew

The morpheme *še-* is used in MH to subordinate a great number of sentential clauses which do not appear, on the surface, as verb complements. In a number of those the underlying relative-clause is quite apparent from the presence of a head-noun classifying the construction, a noun which is always given in the genitive form. One may thus view this pattern as a direct, natural extension of the use of *ʔašer* as a relative subordinator in EBH. Some examples of this are:

6.1.1. PURPOSE CLAUSES

(55) *kdey še-loʔ yaku ʔiš b-reᶜey-hu* (Zr., Peʔa, 4.4)
reason-of THAT-no they-hit man at-friend-his
'so that they don't hit each other'

(56) *ᶜal mnat še-ylaqeṭ bna ʔaḥarav* (Zr., Peʔa, 5.6)
on reason-of THAT-will-gather son-his after-him
'in order that his son will gather after him'

(57) *bi-švil še-loʔ yoʔvedu* (Zr., Dmey, 3.3)
on-way-of THAT-no they-get-lost
'in order that they don't get lost'

6.1.2. SUBJUNCTIVE COMPLEMENTS

(58) *ha-madir ʔet ḥavero še-loʔ yoʔxal* (Zr., Dmey, 4.4)
the-enjoining friend-his THAT-no he-eat
'he who enjoins his friend not to eat'

(59) *din še-loʔ yhu šixḥah* (Zr., Peʔa, 6.6)
law THAT-no it-be leftover
'it is judged that it should not be considered a leftover'

(60) *hitqinu še-yihyu ʔomrim* (Zr., Braxot, 8.7)
they-decreed THAT-they-be saying
'it was decreed that they should say'

(61) *vʔomer: yhi rason še-teled ben zaxar* (Zr., Peʔa, 2.2)
and-says: be-it will THAT-she-bear son male
'and he says: "May it be that she bear a male child"'

6.1.3. IN-SPITE-OF CLAUSES

(62) *ʔaf ᶜal pi še-ʔen ha-baqar yaxol laᶜavor* (Zr., Peʔa, 2.2)
also on mouth-of THAT-no the-cattle can to-pass
'even though the cattle cannot pass'

6.1.4. 'BECAUSE' CLAUSES

(63) *še-ʔen šixḥa ʔelaʔ bi-šᶜat ha-ᶜomer* (Zr., Peʔa, 4.5)
THAT-no leftover except in-hour-of the-harvest
'because there's no leftover except during the harvest'

(64) *še-ken derex bney mlaxin* (Zr., Braxot, 1.7)
THAT-so way-of sons-of kings
'since this is the way of sons of kings'

(65) *še-ᶜavarta ᶜal divrat beyt Hilel* (Zr., Braxot, 1.9)
THAT-you-transgressed on word-of house-of Hillel
'since you have transgressed against the canon of the house of Hillel'

(66) *mi-pney* *še-ʔefšar* (Zr., Peʔa, 5.3)
from-face-of THAT-possible
'because it is possible'

6.1.5. DISCUSSION

From the data presented above two patterns are reasonably apparent:

(a) THE SUBJUNCTIVE PATTERN: Here *še-* is used as a subordinator for sentences in a (semantic) subjunctive environment, whether subordinated by a verb of wishing/manipulating or only inferred. Though there is no shred of a head-of-construction, the semantic similarity between PURPOSE-CLAUSE and SUBJUNCTIVE should be noted, since this may quite likely be the analogy-channel through which *še-* began its spreading from the relativization paradigm.

(b) RELATIVE-RELATED PATTERNS: In the PURPOSE, BECAUSE and IN-SPITE-OF clauses above the erstwhile relative pattern is clearly evident from the presence of a genitival noun, the head (and semantic classifier) of these constructions. What one sees in the 'because' clauses is the growing tendency to dispense with that head noun and leave the clause subordinated by *še-* alone. It is more than likely that the same process of simplification was involved in the presumed development of subjunctive clauses from purpose clauses.

6.2. Verb Complementation in Late Biblical Hebrew

It is hard to imagine, at least initially, why the phonologically-motivated contraction of *ʔašér* into *šé-* and the semantically-syntactically motivated invasion of *ʔašer/še-* into the verb-complement paradigm should be related or occur simultaneously. Nevertheless it is true that in the very same book of the Old Testament (Ecclesiastes) where one finds *ʔašer* and *še-* in a most conspicuous free variation, one also finds a similar free variation between the old verb complementizer *ki* and *ʔašer/še-*. There are reasons to believe that the syntactic-semantic processes by which *ʔašer/še-* was eventually propelled into the V-Comp predated the contraction of *ʔašer* into *še-*.

6.2.1. OCCURRENCES OF ŠE- IN LBH

Scanning through a number of late books, one finds first the sporadic occurrence of *še-*, but only in relative clauses:

JONAH:	REL:	1
	V-Comp:	Ø
CHRONICLES:	REL:	1
	V-Comp:	Ø
EZRA:	REL:	1
	V-Comp:	Ø

Then, in ECCLESIASTES, one finds complete free variation between *še-* and *ʔašer* in both relative clauses and verb complements:

	ʔašer	*še-*
REL:	69	62
V-COMP:	11	12

Finally, in the language of SONG OF SOLOMON the transition from *ʔašer* to *še-* had already been completed:

	ʔašer[12]	*še-*
REL:	Ø	25
V-Comp:	Ø	6

6.2.2. THE USE OF ʔAŠER IN SUBJUNCTIVE COMPLEMENTS IN LBH

In many of the minor prophets and late books in LBH one finds the use of *ʔašer* in subjunctive complements, purpose clauses and 'because' clauses, much like *še-* is used in Mishnaic Hebrew (see section 6.1. above). In many instances it is impossible to formally distinguish between the 'subjunctive' and 'purpose/in order to' usage. Further, in many other instances, in particular where a sentential complement follows a COERCIVE-MANIPULATIVE verb (for a formal definition of those, see Givón, 1973), such as 'order', 'tell', 'request' etc., a formal distinction between a subjunctive and non-subjunctive complement is not possible either. These two distinct processes, the semantic neutralization of 'purpose clause' and 'subjunctive' and the syntactic neutralization of subjunctive and non-subjunctive complements of manipulative verbs, may have played a crucial role in motivating the invasion of *ʔašer* into the V-Comp paradigm. Some representative examples from the late books are:

(67) *va-yoʔmar ha-tiršhaʔ lahem ʔašer loʔ yoʔxlu* (Ezra, 2.63)
and-said the-minister to-them THAT no they-eat
'and the minister told them that they shouldn't eat'

(68) *va-yašem daniʔel ʕal libo ʔašer loʔ* (Dan., 1.8)
and-put Daniel on heart-his THAT no
'and Daniel made sure that

yigaʕel b-fat-bag ha-melex
he-dirty-himself with-bread-of the king
he should not defile himself with the king's food'

(69) *va-yvaqeš mi-šar ha-sarisim ʔašer loʔ yigaʕel* (Dan., 1.9)
and-he-asked from-chief-of the-eunuchs THAT no he-defile-himself
'and he asked of the chief of eunuchs that he not be defiled'

(70) *va-yimṣaʔ katuv ba-torah ʔašer ṣivah YHWH* (Nehem., 8.14)
and-he-found written in-the-Torah THAT ordered God
'and he found written in the Torah that God had ordered

b-yad mošeh ʔašer yešvu bney yišraʔel ba-sukot
in-hand-of Moses THAT they-sit sons-of Israel in-huts
through Moses that the children of Israel should sit in huts'

In (70) above the first occurrence of *ʔašer* is not as a subordinator of a subjunctive complement but rather of 'write'. The use of *ʔašer* is thus clearly spreading from subjunctive to non-subjunctive verb complements. Further:

(71) *vaʔomrah ʔašer loʔ yiftx-um* (Neh., 13.19)
and-I-said THAT no they-open-them
'and I said that they shouldn't open them

ʕad ʔaxar ha-šabat
till after-of the-sabbath
until after the Sabbath'

(72) *va-ʔomrah la-nviʔim ʔašer yihyu miṭṭaharim u-vaʔim* (Neh., 13.22)
and-I-said to-the-prophets THAT they-be cleansing and-coming
'and I told the prophets that they should cleanse themselves and come'

(73) *va-yikkatev... ʔašer loʔ tavoʔ vašti li-fney ha-melex* (Est., 1.19)
and-it-was-written... THAT no come Vashti to-face-of the-king
'and it was written that Vashti should not come in front of the king'

---

[12]The only occurence of *ʔaser* in Song-of-Solomon is extraneous to the text itself, since it appears in the introductory line:

šir ha-širim ʔAŠER *li-šlomoh* (Song, 1.1)
song-of the-songs THAT to-Solomon
'song of songs of Solomon'

(74) *ki mordexay ṣivah ᶜaley-ha ᵓašer loᵓ tagid* (Est., 2,11)
for Mordechai ordered on-her THAT no she-say
'because Mordechai ordered her not to tell'

In the examples above (with one exception noted, (70) the utterance verbs involved were largely MANIPULATIVE verbs, i.e. command or request for action. These verbs are the natural environment for subjunctive complementation. It can be shown, however, that the spread of *ᵓašer* into COGNITION/INFORMATION verb complements is also attested in LBH.

6.2.3. THE USE OF *ᵓašer* IN COMPLEMENTS OF COGNITION VERBS

In addition to (70) above, one also finds the following examples:

(75) *ki higid la-hem ᵓašer huᵓ yhudi* (Est., 3.4)
for he-told to-them THAT he jew
'because he told them that he was a Jew'

(76) *rᵓeh draxey-ha ve-ḥaxam ᵓašer ᵓen lah qaṣin* (Pro., 5.6)
see ways-hers and-wise THAT no to-her officer
'see her ways and wise up, that she has no officers'

(77) *yodᶜim ᵓašer kol ᵓiš ve-ᵓišah* (Est., 4.11)
knowing THAT all man and-woman
'know that every man and woman'

(78) *va-yimmaṣeᵓ katuv ᵓašer higid mordexay ᶜal bigtanaᵓ* (Est., 6.2)
and-was-found written THAT told Mordechai on Bigtana
'and it was found written that Mordechai told on Bigtana'

Further, in Ecclesiastes one finds that *ᵓašer/še-* has long gone on its way toward completely replacing the old subordinator *ki-* (and the more marginal *ve-hineh*). Thus, the distribution of all these subordinators in the indirect-quote paradigm is:

ᵓašer	11
še-	12
ki	11
vehineh	1

The new subordinator pattern thus outnumbers the old one two to one. And in Song of Solomon all 6 occurences of indirect-quote verb complements are subordinated by *še-*, with no trace of *ki/vehineh*. This is the same situation as in MH. Some representative examples of the V-Comp pattern from thses two books are:

(79) *ṭov ᵓašer tidor mi-še-tidor ve-loᵓ tšalem* (Eccl., 5.4)
good THAT you-promise from-THAT-you-promise and-no you-pay
'it is better to promise than to promise and not pay'

(80) *yadaᶜti še-gam huᵓ rᶜut ruaḥ* (Eccl., 1.17)
I-knew THAT-too he folly-of spirit
'I knew that it too was folly'

(81) *v-li-rᵓot še-hem bhemah* (Eccl., 9.19)
and-to-see THAT-they beast
'and to see that they are beasts'

(82) *ᵓal tirᵓu-ni še-ᵓani šharḥoret* (Song of S., 1.6)
don't you-see-me THAT-I dark
'do not see (me) that I am dark'

(83) *mah tagido lo, še-ḥolat ᵓahavah ᵓani* (Song of S., 5.9)
what you-will-tell to-him, THAT-sick-of love I
'What will you tell him? That I'm lovesick'

One should also note that the use of *ᵓašer/še-* as subordinator of 'because' clauses is also attested in these two books, albeit meagerly:

(84) *pitḥi li... še-ro?ši nimla? ṭal* (Song of S., 5.2)
open to-me... THAT-head-my filled dew
'open to me...since my head is full of dew'

(85) *mah dodex mi-dod še-kaxah hišba^ctanu* (Song of S., 5.11)
what lover-your from-lover THAT-thus you-enjoined-us
'what makes your lover so special that you've thus enjoined us?'

(86) *b-še-l ?ašer ya^camol* (Eccl., 8.17)
in-THAT-to THAT he-will-toil
'because he toils'

The evidence thus suggests rather clearly that the books of Ecclesiastes and Song of Solomon, in that order, represent the more progressive dialect layer in the Old Testament. Further, the invasion of *?ašer/še-* into the V-Comp paradigm seems to have been already completed in Late Biblical Hebrew. In the next section I will discuss another intermediate syntactic pattern which, I believe, contributed to the complex syntactic/semantic changes which brought about the introduction of *?ašer/še-* into verb complements.

6.3. The Relative-Accusative Blend in Verb Complements

In the preceding sections I have suggested that there are reasons to believe that the semantic similarity of PURPOSE and SUBJUNCTIVE clauses may have motivated at least one pathway through which *?ašer/še-* spread from relative clauses to verb complements. In this section I would like to outline another intermediate syntactic pattern which, I believe, has considerable bearing on this diachronic change. I will further show that this pattern dates back to EBH.

To begin with, note that all verbs of utterance and cognition which take SENTENTIAL complements also take—and so far as I know this is true of all languages—NOMINAL complements. And those come in the accusative-object case. Now, in both EBH and LBH there exists a pattern, in complements of the indirect-quote type, which is clearly a BLEND between a sentential and accusative-nominal complement of cognition verbs. And in this syntactic blend (or 'syntactic intermediate'), the relative subordinator *?ašer/še-* figures most conspicuously. Though in a few instances the V-Comp subordinator *ki* is involved instead. A few examples, first from LBH, will illustrate this pattern:

(87) *r?eh ?et ma^cašeh ha-?elohim ki mi yuxal* (Eccl., 7.13)
see ACC deed-of the-God THAT who can
'behold the acts of God (and) that who could

ltaqen ?et ?ašer ^civt-o
repair ACC that he-twisted-it
repair what He ruined'

(88) *v-ra?iti ?et kol he-^camal... ki hi? qin^cat* (Eccl., 4.4)
and-I-saw ACC all the-toil... THAT she envy-of
'and I saw all the toil...(and) that it breeds envy

?iš me-re^ce-hu
man from-friend-his
among men'

(89) *?al tir?u-ni še-?ani šharḥoret* (Song of S., 1.6)
don't you-see-me THAT-I dark
'do not see that I am dark'

(90) *va-ysaper la-hem Haman... v-?et kol* (Est., 5.11)
and-told to-them Haman... and-ACC all
'and Haman told them...and all

?ašer gidl-o ha-melex
THAT increased-him the-king
(about) that the king honored him'

(91) ...*v-ʔet ʔašer niśʔ-o ʕal ha-śarim* (Est., 5.11)
...and-ACC THAT he-raised-him above the-ministers
'...and (about) that he raised him over the (other) ministers'

(92) *mah še-hayah kvar niqraʔ šm-o v-nodaʕ* (Eccl., 6.11)
what that-was already was-called name-his and-known
'whatever has passed has already been told and known

va-ʔašer huʔ ʔadam
and-THAT he man
that he's a man'

As was shown earlier, in LBH the subordinator *ʔašer/še-* had already invaded the V-Comp paradigm. So that the accusative-sentential complement 'blend', while suggestive, is not as pivotal. However, the same pattern is also found in EBH, where again, in a number of instances, it is 'blended' with the old V-Comp subordinators *ki/vehineh:*

(93) *va-yarʔ ʔelohim ʔet ha-ʔor ki ṭov* (Gen., 1.4)
and-saw God ACC the-light THAT good
'and God saw the light/that it was good'

(94) *va-yarʔ ʔelohim ʔet kol ʔašer ʕasah vehineh ṭov* (Gen., 1.31)
and-saw God ACC all that he-made AND-LO good
'and God saw all that he made/that it was good'

(95) *šamaʕnu ʔet ʔašer hoviš YHWH ʔet mey yam suf* (Josh., 2.10)
we-heard ACC THAT dried Yhwh ACC water-of sea-of Suf
'we heard that God had dried up the Red Sea's water

(96) *va-ʔamartem la-hem ʔašer nixrtu mey ha-yarden* (Josh., 4.7)
and-you-told to-them THAT stopped water-of the-Jordan
'and you tell them that the Jordan's water stopped'

(97) *va-yoʔmer leʔmor: ʔašer yišʔalun bney-xem mahar* (Josh., 4.21)
and-said saying: THAT will-ask sons-your tomorrow
'and he said: if your sons will ask you tomorrow'

(98) *va-yhi ki-šmoʕa... ʔet ʔašer hoviš YHWH* (Josh., 5.1)
and-be when-hearing... ACC THAT dried Yhwh
'and so when (they) heard that Yhwh dried up...'

(99) *hugad l-ʕavd-xa ʔet ʔašer ṣivah YHWH ʔelohey-xa* (Josh., 9.24)
was-told to-slave-your ACC THAT ordered Yhwh God-your
'it was told to your servant that Yhwh your God

ʔet mošeh latet la-xem ʔet kol ha-ʔareṣ
ACC Moses to-give to-you ACC all the-land
ordered Moses to give you the whole land'

With respect to blends such as (99) for example, one is tempted to suggest that the speaker was really hedging, first aiming to say:

(100) '*We heard* THAT WHICH *Jehovah ordered Moses*'

that is, a NOMINAL complement. But then changing his mind in mid-speech and adding the actual proposition/contents of God's mandate, i.e.:

(101) '*Namely* THAT *Jehovah ordered Moses to give you...*'

Another blend pattern may be seen in:

(102) *diber YHWH ʔet ha-davar ha-zeh el mošeh* (Josh., 14.10)
said Yhwh ACC the-thing the-this to Moses
'God said this thing to Moses

ʔašer halax yišraʔel
THAT went Israel
that Israel went'

Here, it seems, the speaker first aims at direct-quote citation:

(103) '*God told* THIS THING *to Moses*: "..."'

Then, in mid-stream, the speaker decided to opt for indirect-quote. His strategy is then to RELATIVIZE the contents of the quoted proposition (i.e. the sentential complement) to the co-referent *this thing*, i.e.:

(104) '*The thing* (*that God said to Moses*) (*was*) THAT...'

I believe this is a highly NATURAL explanation for the appearance of blends of this type. The universal property of cognition verbs, of taking both sentential and nominal complements, enhances the naturalness of this suggestion. Note also that the nominal complement of cognition verbs is most often a NOMINALIZATION OF A SENTENTIAL COMPLEMENT, a factor that enhances the identity between the two and thus facilitates the blend. Note also that COUNTERPARTS of blends of this type are found when sentences with cognition verbs and sentential complements are nominalized. The product of this nominalization is a noun-phrase in which the erstwhile V-Comp appears as a relative clause—subordinated by the same subordinator used in the V-Comp, as in:

(105) '*He knew* THAT *she was right*' → '*His knowledge* THAT *she was right*'

While the process depicted in (105) above is of the opposite directionality with respect to the subordinator (that is, it would presumably change V-Comp subordinators into relative subordinators), it nevertheless enhances the suggested identification of a sentential quoted proposition with a nominal complement of a cognition verb. Finally, the role of hedges or 'afterthoughts' of a similar sort in syntactic change has been recently argued by Hyman (1974).

To sum up this section, then, it was shown that a second channel exists through which the subordinator *ʔašer/še-* could have been transmitted from its original relative-clause environment into V-Comp paradigms. It was further shown that intermediates or 'blends' of this second type appeared in both EBH and LBH. It should also be noted, to conclude this section, that the first channel of transmission, i.e. the subjunctive/purpose pattern, is already discernible in EBH, as in:

(106) *ha-yom ha-ze ʔaḥel gadel-xa b-ᶜeyney kol yišraʔel* (Josh., 3.7)
the-day the-this I-start increase-you in-eyes-of all Israel
'this day I shall begin to raise you in the eyes of all Israel

ʔašer yedᶜu ki ka-ʔašer hayiti ᶜim Mošeh
THAT they-know that like I-was with Moses
so that they know that the way I was with Moses'

7. DISCUSSION

7.1. Biblical Dialects and Biblical Chronology

I think one should resist deriving facile conclusions from the dialect variation described above as to the relative chronology of Old Testament books. The level of formality and severity of editorial interference in the various books make chronologies of this kind rather frustrating to predict. One could clearly suggest, however, that with respect to the syntax of relativization and verb complementation, it is possible to identify a dialect progression within Biblical Hebrew, roughly of the following order:

(107) EARLY: Genesis, Joshua, Judges (and others)
LATER: Ezra, Nehemiah, Esther (probably some others)
LATER: Ecclesiastes
LATEST: Song of Solomon

The latter, Song of Solomon, reflects the syntactic situation found in Mishnaic Hebrew. It may well be that in popular speech this progressive dialect existed much much earlier than Biblical attestation. The fact that Song of Solomon is, most likely, a popular erotic text which had been later re-christened as a presumed religious allegory, may explain the much more progressive dialect found in it. Similar considerations may or may not hold true for Ecclesiastes.

7.2. Analogy vs. Internal Natural Change

I think the data discussed above strongly suggest that the analogy hypothesis in this case is both undesirable and unnecessary. Two independent patterns of syntactic change seem to have converged in this case. They may be summarized as:

(i) The semantic similarity between PURPOSE CLAUSES, (which are constructed via the relative pattern with *ʔašer/še-*) and SUBJUNCTIVES, together with the fact that verbs requiring subjunctive complements may also be verbs of utterance taking (direct and) indirect-quote sentential complements, led to the introduction of *ʔašer/še-* first into indirect-quote complements of utterance verbs ('tell', 'order', 'ask') and then presumably onward through the paradigm to cognition verbs ('know', 'see', 'remember', 'understand', 'hear'). This transition may have been facilitated by an extension, observed independently, of indirect-quote complements into utterance-verb paradigms.

(ii) Syntactic intermediates or 'blends' between an accusative-nominal and a sentential complement of cognition verbs seem to be independently responsible for the introduction of *ʔašer/še-* into the V-Comp paradigm. The fact that all verbs involved here take both nominal(ized) and sentential complements certainly enhances the possibility of blends of this type occuring.

I would like then to suggest that one need not view the shift involved here as a result of a single cause, but rather as arising from the convergence of two independent causes. This certainly enhances the plausibility that the change was a specific, internally-motivated one rather than the outcome of 'mere' analogy. The fact that all the considerations related to both changes are of a highly universal nature further enhances the plausibility of this hypothesis. It also enhances the possibility that other languages where a DEMONSTRATIVE (etymologically) appears as the subordinator for both relative clauses and V-Comp's, such as Akkadian, Aramaic and others, have followed similar routes in spreading the relative subordinator into the V-Comp paradigm.

7.3. Borrowing vs. Internal Natural Change

One may still argue that the spreading of *ʔašer/še-* into the V-Comp paradigm was a result of borrowing. In this section I would like to consider two possible sources.

7.3.1. ANALOGICAL BORROWING FROM ARAMAIC

In Biblical (and later) Aramaic one finds the erstwhile DEMONSTRATIVE *di* functioning as both a relative clause and V-Comp subordinator. One may thus argue that during the time where *ʔašer/še-* spread into the V-Comp environment, Aramaic was already the prevalent sub-stratum language and perhaps the extension from relative to V-Comp subordinator was done by analogy with Aramaic. I think this hypothesis is not particularly attractive. To begin with, I have shown that two separate internal, natural developments within Biblical Hebrew created strong pressures toward the extension of *ʔašer/še-* to V-Comp environments. Since a much more specific explanation is available, it seems to me that a simplistic recourse to borrowing should be rejected. Further, Rosen (1959) has shown that a pattern equivalent to that with *di* in Aramaic is marginally attested in Biblical Hebrew. It is found only in Poetic, Exhortative, set-pattern texts and involves the morpheme *zu*, an erstwhile demonstrative which lost its gender/number agreement. Thus, for example:

(108) *ʿam zu gaʔalta* (Exodus, 15.13)
people THAT you-saved
'the people that you saved'

(109) *brešet zu ṭamnu nilkda raglam* (Psalms, 9.16)
in-net THAT they-layed was-caught foot-their
'in the net that they spread their own foot got snared'

(110) *bi-mzimotay zu hašavti* (Psalms, 10.2)
in-plots-my THAT I-planned
'in the plots that I conceived'

(111) *v-ʔorexa* *b-derex* *zu* *telex* (Psalms, 32.8)
and-I-guide-you in-way THAT you-go
'and I shall guide you in the way in which you go'

While Rosen (1959) cites a number of examples where it is not clear whether *zu* is a relative subordinator or a demonstrative modifying the head noun, in (108)-(111) above its function is unambiguously that of a relative subordinator. This shows that an identical pattern to that of Aramaic existed in Pre-EBH, but it was confined only to relative clauses, did not spread into verb complements, and in general did not spread much or at least did not survive in anything but relic contexts in EBH. This makes it so much less plausible that Biblical Hebrew would have borrowed this pattern from Aramaic.

7.3.2. BORROWING (OR 'SURVIVAL') FROM AKKADIAN

It has been suggested that the LBH and MH morpheme *še-* is a survival from the Akkadian *ša-*, which functions both as a relative and V-Comp subordinator. I think this suggestion is extremely implausible. To begin with, *ša-* is attested only at one spot (twice) in the Old Testament—in Song of Deborah, as:

(112) *ʕad* *ša-qamti* *dvorah,* *ša-qamti* *ʔem* *b-yišraʔel* (Judges, 5.7)
till THAT-I-rose Deborah, THAT -I-rose mother in-Israel
'until I, Debora rose, I, mother in Israel'

The language of this text is by itself one of the most petrified anachronistic levels in the Old Testament. Further, while EBH is clearly a literary dialect, it nevertheless represents a language that was spoken at some previous time. It seems to me that it is rather inconceivable that the Akkadian-like *ša-/še-* had gone underground and remained submerged for a period covering the linguistic span from Genesis all the way to Ecclesiastes, and then re-surface some 1,000 odd years later.

In addition, note that the contraction of *ʔašer-* to *šé-* is highly natural in Hebrew phonology, given the final stress, the grammaticalization of an erstwhile noun and its gradually evolving PREFIXAL status. The reduced *še-* is itself a prefix. The scribal orthography of the Old Testament strongly suggests that perhaps *ʔašer* was already a bound prefix even before its reduction. The loss of an initial syllable with no stress, especially with as weak a consonant as /ʔ/ (Aleph), is extremely plausible. The borrowing hypothesis is then rather unnecessary.

Finally, one should point out (for details see Rosen, 1959) that closely related dialects, Canaanite and Phoenician, had a similar relative subordinator. It most often appears as the REDUCED *ʔš*, but in a limited number of contexts it is still attested as the full form *ʔšr*. While the reduction in Phoenician may have not gone the entire way as in LBH and MH, the loss of /*r*/—via a highly natural assimilatory or cluster-simplifying rule (or both)—is nevertheless shared by Phoenician and Hebrew. The Akkadian borrowing hypothesis is thus all the less attractive.

7.4. Why was the Old Early Biblical Hebrew Verb-Complement Subordinator Lost?

I have shown earlier that EBH had TWO indirect-quote subordinator, *ki* and the more margianl *vehineh*. It is thus legitimate to ask why they were so completely replaced by LBH. While I have no final answer to this, a number of factors may be considered.

To begin with, within EBH itself *ki* had clearly won over *vehineh*. In the first 34 chapters of Genesis the ration *ki*:*vehineh* is 29:12. In the combined first 20 chapters of Joshua and of Judges the ratio is 20:4. On the other hand, *ki* itself is extensively used in EBH as a 'because' subordinator, as it is also used in MH. It may thus well be that the availability of the extended *še-* relieved *ki* of its double function, i.e. that lexical re-alignment had occured because of SUPPLETION. This may be supported by the following argument: As we have seen earlier, in LBH the indirect-quote pattern had been extended to UTTERANCE verbs (whereas in EBH it was confined to cognition verbs). Now, since *ki* was still used extensively in LBH as a 'because' morpheme, subordinating sentences, then any time one wished to say a sentence auch as:

(113) *'and he said:* "BECAUSE *you did this...*"'

an ambiguity would have been created, automatically, between the direct-quote interpretation in (113) and an alternative INDIRECT-quote:

(114) *'and he said* THAT *you did this...'*

While this is by no means a proof, it is nevertheless a rather plausible suggestion, especially that an alternative subordinator, *ʔašer/še-*, was already available.

REFERENCES

Givón, T. (1973) "The time-axis phenomenon", *Language*, 49.4:890-925

——— (1974) "Serial verbs and syntactic change: Niger-Congo", in C. Li (ed.), *Proceedings of Conference on word-order and word-order change*, (Santa Barbara, January 1974), Austin: Texas University Press (to appear)

Hyman, L. (1974) "On the change from SOV to SVO: Evidence from Niger-Congo", in C. Li (ed.) (see above)

Rosen, H. (1959) "Zur Vorgeschichte des Relativsatzes im Nordwest-semitischen", *Archív Orientální*, 27:186-198

MONOGRAPHIC JOURNALS OF THE NEAR EAST

General Editor: Giorgio Buccellati

MJNE is a system of journals on the Near East, with each journal devoted to a specialized study area, and each issue consisting of a single article.

General Subscription

For a prepayment of $10 the subscriber selects random issues from within the entire system as desired, up to a total of 200 pages. The subscriber is also entitled to (1) periodical lists of abstracts from all journals in the system, and (2) reservation to any journal within the system, whereby issues of a given journal are sent on approval immediately upon publication (and may be returned within two weeks).

Library Subscription

A prepayment of $10 for each journal in the system secures all issues of a single volume as soon as they are published. This subscription schedule does not allow the selection of random issues; in return, a discount is provided in the form of a greater number of pages for the basic price of $10 (since a volume will normally include more than 200 pages).

Payment must accompany orders from individuals. A handling fee of 70¢ will be charged to Libraries if order is not prepaid. Order from: UNDENA PUBLICATIONS, P.O.Box 97, Malibu, California 90265, U.S.A.

AFROASIATIC LINGUISTICS

AAL includes contributions in linguistics within the vast domain of Afroasiatic (Hamito-Semitic) languages. Articles of general, theoretical interest using Afroasiatic material, descriptive, historical and comparative studies are included.

Editor: Robert Hetzron (1346 San Rafael, Santa Barbara, Ca. 93109 U.S.A.)
Advisory Board: A. Ambros, A. Bloch, J. B. Callender, T. Givón, T. G. Penchoen, S. Segert

Volume 1
Issue 1: P. Newman & R. G. Schuh, *The Hausa Aspect System,* 38 pp.

In this paper the authors hope to account for the aspect marking constructions of modern Hausa by providing detailed historical explanations of their origin and development, beginning with morphological forms and syntactic patterns reconstructed for Proto-Hausa. The description accounts for the asymmetry in certain paradigms, the lack of parallelism between affirmative and negative paradigms in certain aspects, and some of the differences between contemporary dialects. The hypotheses about Hausa history are supported by reliable comparative data from other Chadic languages.

Issue 2: J. L. Malone, *The Development of the Anomalous Syriac Verb eškāḥ 'To Find': A Case of Convergent Factors in Linguistic Change,* 10 pp.

The canonically anomalous shape of the Syriac Verb *eškáḥ* 'to find' is shown to result from a convergence of diachronic pressures on an intersection of phonological weak spots and morpho-syntactic defectiveness for moderate phonological anomaly. The developmental hypothesis adopted underscores the importance both of multiple factors in diachronic change and of homeostasis in linguistic systems.

Issue 3: R. Hetzron, *Extrinsic Ordering in Classical Arabic,* 25 pp.

One speaks of extrinsic ordering when the order of application of two rules must be specifically indicated and does not follow from a general principle. In Arabic the survival of a long vowel in a syllable made closed by a contraction may be a case of such ordering, though it may also be interpreted as an intrinsically ordered sequel of 'nonproductive–operative' rules. On the other hand, the incongruent agreement of numerals with the underlying singulars of the co-occurring plural nouns is definitely extrinsically ordered.